A window on WEYBRIDGE

including St George's Hill & Oatlands

D.M. & J.L. BARKER

Introduction

Although much development has taken place in recent years, the Weybridge area has retained many of the features which give it its own distinctive character. We hope that the opening of this particular window on Weybridge will prove once again that the photographic image plays a vital part in helping to record aspects of the recent past.

As with our previous work, we have attempted to arrange the contents in a topographical sequence. This has allowed us to illustrate the development of the original village and parish of Weybridge, the strong influence of local waterways on its situation, and the later effects of the break-up of local estates to form the current townscape.

In order to cover what may be regarded as the present extent of the town, it was felt necessary to include the St. George's Hill and Oatlands areas, parts of which anciently belonged to the adjoining parishes of Byfleet and Walton-on-Thames. The area covered by the track at Brooklands has, however, been excluded from this particular collection. While the site greatly influenced and continues to affect the Weybridge area, its own special history is well illustrated in other publications.

Weybridge and district has been blessed with a succession of fine amateur and professional photographers who have left an invaluable record of many aspects of past activity. Examples of some of the best of their work are presented here in what we hope is a fitting tribute to their craft.

Further reproductions of Victorian and Edwardian photographs of the area are to be found in two excellent books: the Elmbridge Museum publication 'Camera Studies' by Morag Barton and the recent paper published by the Walton and Weybridge Local History Society, 'A Short History of Weybridge' by M. E. Blackman and J. S. L. Pulford. The Society, as well as holding regular meetings has, since its inception 30 years ago, under its motto 'To learn about the past', consistently published the results of its members' research into a wide range of local historical subjects. We also gratefully acknowledge the help and facilities for research offered by Elmbridge Museum, whose own collections dating back to 1906 reflect the continuing commitment of local government to the preservation and display of our local history.

David and Jocelyn Barker
November 1993

Front Cover

Centre: The Monument c.1912, erected in 1822 in memory of the Duchess of York.
Left: Queens Road c.1910; St. George's Hill golf course under construction c.1912; The Grotto Inn, Monument Hill, c.1910.
Right: Portmore Pillars, Thames Street, c.1910; Upper chamber of the Grotto, Oatlands Park, c.1910; Baker Street looking west c.1910.

Thames Lock c.1900

Captured by the camera of Thomas Griffin, the High Street photographer, a fully-laden barge is about to enter Thames Lock. Displayed on the stern are the details of the owners and the Port of London registration number – a reminder of the original commercial importance of the Wey Navigation. Although cargoes had been carried on the River Wey before 1653, its canalization from the Thames to Guildford and later Godalming allowed important industrial sites to develop on its banks. The complex of buildings on the right includes Whittet's Mill and, beside the footbridge, the lock-keeper's cottage occupied at this time by Mr. Grove. Weybridge's Thames Lock was naturally one of the busiest on the Navigation, with a constant stream of horse-drawn barges carrying up to 70 tons of freight to and from various mills and wharfs. Whittet's Mill at this time specialised in the extraction of vegetable oils using steam and water power, but had originally been erected c.1691 as a paper mill.

Lang's Works 1913

Arthur Alexander Dashwood Lang founded his own company in 1913 in partnership with David Ernest Garrett. A native of Weybridge, he had previously headed the propeller department of the Bristol and Colonial Aeroplane Company, which had opened a flying school at Brooklands in September 1910. Lang's first factory was based in the buildings originally used by the Thames Valley Launch Co. Ltd. This company was a major builder of river craft and advertised itself as designers and constructors of launches, sailing boats and houseboats. They seem to have specialised in electric launches and under their Managing Director W. Rowland Edwards A.M.I.E.E. maintained a fleet of 40 of these craft. Lang's choice of the old boat building works also gave him a skilled workforce used to bending and laminating timber, which was the basis of the early propeller industry. Later used by the Airscrew Company, the building burnt down in 1942.

The Camps, Hamhaugh Island c.1912

Although administratively and geographically linked to the Middlesex bank of the Thames, Hamhaugh Island is also closely linked to the growth and development of Weybridge. Prior to the arrival of summer campers, the island had been a hay meadow leased from the Ecclesiastical Commissioners by George Dunton, the Shepperton and Weybridge boat builder. Originally, campers rented spaces to erect tents during the summer months and were not allowed permanent structures. Many of these original holiday residents came from the London area for weekends, bringing tents and other gear by road or rail to Shepperton or Weybridge Station. These first campers, staying for a few weeks after the hay was cut, gradually increased in number until the island had annual residents from Easter to September. After the first World War, George Dunton's son Jack sold the occupiers these plots, which were gradually built on with bungalows of various types, although two families seem to have used tents until c.1938. Whilst allowing a taste of country life, it was also necessary to have good boating skills, as access to the island was only possible with their own craft or using the Shepperton or Weybridge ferries. The campers also involved themselves with the Weybridge Regatta. Amy Gentry's family were early residents, and she went on to help found the Weybridge Ladies' Amateur Rowing Club.

The Thames 1947

Weybridge's position at the confluence of the Rivers Wey and Thames left it vulnerable to the floods which affect the Thames Valley. Most Thameside parishes had areas of fertile meadowland which actually relied on the regular spring flood. Climatic changes and the gradual urbanisation of these areas meant that sudden rises in water level caused serious inundations of the riverside areas. The Thames Conservancy had undertaken major works since the beginning of the 19th century in dredging and building locks and weirs to aid navigation and the flow of the river. The flood of 1947 seems, however, to have been the most serious on record, surpassing even the disastrous one of 1894. An unusually severe winter followed by a rapid thaw led to scenes like this throughout the Thames Valley.

Weybridge Ferry 1910

A crossing of the Thames by means of a ferry had linked Weybridge and Shepperton for many centuries. The passage from Thames Street to Ferry Lane on the Middlesex bank was achieved at the time the photograph was taken by means of a heavy punt or skiff, depending on the state of the river. A trip cost a penny (0.4p) and the service ran all day on demand. The boatman who ran the ferry also worked for boatbuilders Dunton's, who had works on both sides of the Thames. It is thought that Mr. Kingham is seen in this photograph, preparing to load pedestrians and cyclists for Shepperton.

Weybridge Sports 12th May 1913

Amateur sport of all kinds developed in the area in the late 19th century, and as well as enjoying the facilities offered by the local rivers and lakes, Weybridge supported a flourishing athletics club. The early history of the club is still uncertain, although in July 1893 the Weybridge Harriers held a meeting in the grounds of Holstein House. The event of 1913, held at Weybridge Football Ground in Walton Lane, was pronounced a great success, with a big crowd despite the incessant rain, the first to mar the event for seven years. As well as a large and varied programme of track and field events, the annual sports included music, courtesy of the Band of the Royal Horse Guards, and military displays including 'lemon cutting' and 'dummy thrusting'.

Thames Street 1974

These brick and weatherboard cottages just north of the corner of Jessamy Road were an interesting survival of a type of dwelling more usually associated with industrial areas. The cottages were originally connected with the nearby oil seed crushing mills established at Thames Lock in 1842. A survey of 1864 shows that the five cottages and gardens were owned by the then owner of the mill, William Houghton Flintan. Possibly erected by him to house some of his workers, the houses retained the name Flintans or Mill Cottages until their demolition in 1974.

Weybridge Bus Garage, June 1926

Weybridge's first motor bus started running on 23rd May, 1914 following delays caused by trouble in obtaining a licence. The service, operated by Guildford & District Motor Services, ran from Guildford to Walton – a two hour journey. In April 1923, plans were submitted by the London General Omnibus Company for a garage to house six to eight buses at the rear of the Electricity Works between 45 and 47 Thames Street, opposite Grotto Road. The garage opened on 16th May, 1923, the Electricity Works being demolished the same year. In September 1924 the L.G.O.C. were given permission to re-build the temporary structure. The building never housed more than four vehicles inside, and probably two or three on the forecourt. These were initially of the new (in 1923) single-decker 'S' type, and were employed on route 79 (later renumbered 219), which in 1926 ran hourly between Kingston and Woking Station, and on route 61, running hourly from Kingston to Staines. In 1931, Weybridge became the only garage to house the experimental 'CB' type single-deckers, of which only three were built, incorporating the only chassis manufactured by the L.G.O.C. A few 'T' type single-deckers were also based here from about 1931-32. The Weybridge Bus Garage closed on 30th September 1939.

Weybridge & District Laundry c.1930

The Weybridge & District Laundry was situated at no. 47 Thames Street and seems to have been started c.1924 by Alfred Howland, also of Thames Street. An earlier establishment in the same street had been started in 1870 by John Walter Brooker, and traded as the Weybridge Sanitary Laundry. This group of lady employees, including on the left, in the dark dress, Miss Dedman, pose by the firm's delivery lorry. Although powered appliances were becoming more widely available at this time, many households still used the service of a regular collection and delivery in a wicker basket, as shown here doubling as a seat, for their weekly wash.

The King's Arms c. 1903

Licensee Mr. Thomas Mathews and his wife pose outside the old King's Arms, now known as the Farnell Arms. The property seems to be on the site of one of Weybridge's oldest licensed premises and is first recorded as an alehouse in 1729, with John Teame as landlord. By 1832 the premises were in the ownership of the Farnell family, who had acquired the Isleworth Brewery in 1800. In 1892 the clientele were recorded as being 'respectable class and boating people'. Members of the Mathews family were associated with the King's Arms from c.1840 until the death of Mrs. Florence Mathews in 1934. The following year, plans were approved for rebuilding by the Isleworth Brewery, by then a part of Watney Combe Reid & Co. The present building, typical of pub architecture of the mid-1930s, was renamed The Farnell Arms c.1981 after its former owners.

V.E. Party 1945

Although there were no publicly-organised celebrations in Weybridge to mark the end of the War in Europe, local initiative found ways to mark the event. Many areas set up impromptu street parties with food and drink especially for the children. These events are fondly remembered by all the participants, as are the refreshments provided out of heavily-rationed wartime supplies. As well as the party fare, some streets celebrated with other events, such as fancy dress parades, treasure hunts and sports. Church Walk's party was enlivened by the burning of an effigy of Hitler. Here, residents of Dorchester Road and Gascoigne Road have combined to provide a tea, set out in a 'V for Victory' formation.

Council Water Cart c. 1905

Gravel was a universal road-surfacing material at the turn of the century, which iron-shod horse-drawn traffic soon pulverised to grit and dust. Windy weather could quickly raise choking clouds to the general discomfiture of pedestrians and road users alike. To counter this effect, the Local Authority employed water carts to lay the dust, and Weybridge Council's vehicle is seen here in Elm Grove Road. The Council Stables in Elm Grove Road were sold in 1909. The custom in some areas of holding a parade of decorated horses like this one was introduced around 1900, but died out with the start of the first World War. A local resident writing in 1969 recalls the same horse wearing a straw hat with holes cut for his ears during hot sunny weather.

High Street and Church Street c.1898

A local road-sweeper can be seen here resting against the trunk of one of the large trees which once lined both sides of the High Street, with a bottle (possibly containing cold tea) beside him. His broom, together with those of his absent companions, leans against the next tree, while the evidence of their labour lies in neat piles by the kerbs awaiting collection. Behind him is the gate leading to the grounds of Holstein House, while the new London & County Bank is just visible on the near side of Baker Street. On the further corner is Aberdeen House, then occupied by the local butcher, Washington Dale. The butcher's shop continued trading under John Ives from 1906, while the remainder of the building housed the Council Offices from 1908. The view of the Parish Church is uninterrupted either by the present parade of gabled shops erected about 1899 or by the more short-lived row of buildings which preceded them.

Baker Street c.1908

No. 1 High Street has been associated with banking since 1897 when the London & County Bank opened its new premises here on 25th October. As a result of amalgamations and mergers between 1909 and 1968, the business known today as the National Westminster Bank continues to trade from the site. Bank Corner, as it became known, was the scene of a most interesting traffic census in 1909. This was held in support of the local authority's plans to introduce a 10 m.p.h. speed limit in the area. Among the traffic counted on 28th June were 1,749 bicycles, 225 carriages, 20 motor vans, 179 motor cars, two traction engines and a drove of cattle. Apart from revealing much about contemporary road traffic, the survey also illustrated the problems which the new forms of mechanical transport posed for the existing road layout. Baker Street had a width of only 21 ft. at its narrowest and, although widened during the rebuilding of various properties, still retained its basic character as a narrow back street. In the event, the speed limit was introduced, a policeman on point duty at the junction helping to enforce the new safety measure.

National Provincial Bank, 12 High Street, 1936

No. 12 High Street, part of Holstein Parade, had been occupied by a variety of traders prior to the opening of a branch of the National Provincial Bank on 16th April, 1936. Under its Manager, Mr. C.E. Matthews, it was originally open between 10 a.m. and 3 p.m. on weekdays and 9 a.m. and 12 noon on Saturday. The interior view, also taken for the opening, well illustrates the typical up-to-date furnishing of a smaller branch bank, including the blotting pads and pewter inkwells provided before the advent of the ballpoint pen. On the merger of the National Provincial and Westminster Banks in 1978 the branch closed.

The bank's neighbouring premises also housed local branches of national concerns. Boots the chemists had arrived in Weybridge by 1924 and the Home & Colonial by 1909. As well as illustrating the bank's handsome new frontage, the photo also records two contemporary aspects of street life. The flower sellers, who are recorded as obtaining their stock from nurseries near Hampton, had previously had a pitch outside the Newcastle Arms since 1898. Many retailers, and particularly grocers, would routinely offer a regular home delivery service based on trade bikes and youthful muscle power. The Home & Colonial bikes and those of many other shops were a familiar sight until the advent of self-service stores after the Second World War.

Holstein Hall c.1908

Weybridge's Holstein Hall became a dominant feature of the High Street for nearly 60 years. The building was the brainchild of local catering entrepreneur John Wiltshire of the Common. Mr. Wiltshire had bought the Village Hall in Prince's Road for £1,500 in 1901 and continued its use as a local venue for mass meetings and entertainment. In June 1904 the first sod was cut for his new Holstein Hall, to be built in the grounds of Holstein House. Designed by Henry Budd and built by William Mann's company, Weybridge's new hall, with a seating capacity of 900, was opened on 7th January, 1905, with a programme including the Weybridge Choral Society performing Mendelssohn's 'Elijah'. The lavishly decorated hall rapidly became the venue for many varied entertainments and functions. As well as attracting top London artistes, including Albert ('My Old Dutch') Chevalier and the 'Imperial Bioscope', a hand-cranked moving picture show, the hall also had a dance floor. This feature, of sprung pine, was reputed to be the best in the South of England. After initial success, the venture seemed to lose favour with the local population. Contemporary memoirs record that the local gentry began to use the new facilities available on St. George's Hill after 1913 which, together with the arrival of permanent cinemas in neighbouring towns, helped to cause the hall's decline.

Wood's Garage c.1927

Early in 1917, the Holstein Hall was purchased by Vickers as a subsidiary works for their Brooklands aeroplane factories. Following the conclusion of the first World War, the building remained empty until 1923, when it was purchased for use as a billiard hall by Douglas Cleland. This venture does not seem to have actively taken off and in July of 1923 Holstein Hall was sold to Samuel Howard Wood, who had been operating a garage next door at no. 24 High Street since c.1912. The hall was fitted out as a car showroom and opened for business in May 1924. Unfortunately, Mr. Wood died later that year, but the business was carried on by members of his family. In 1927 a convoy of 14 Buicks arrived here to demonstrate the quality of nine Hendon-built Fisher bodies and five examples of English and Van den Plas bodywork to the car buyers of Weybridge.

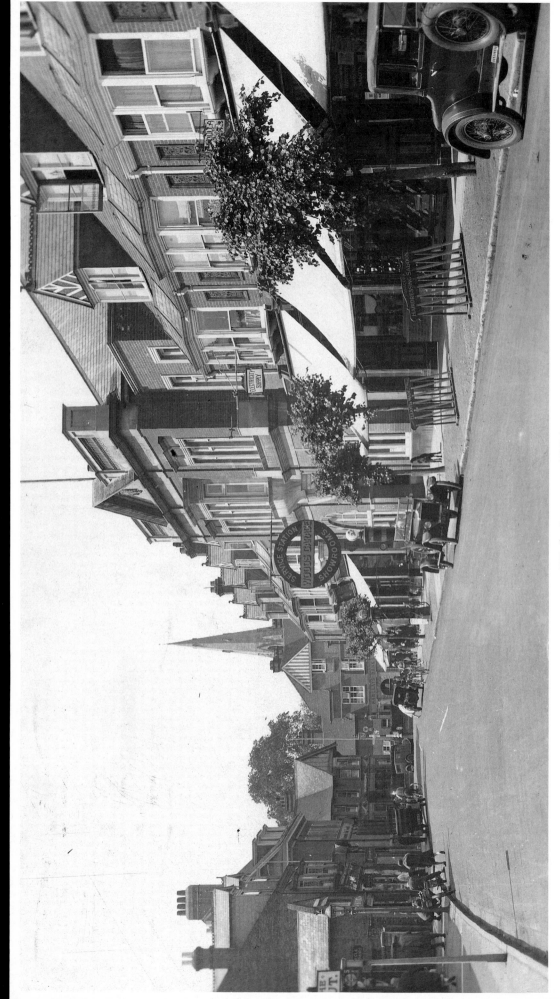

High Street c.1931

Wood's Garage sign dominated the street scene at this time. Today's planning regulations would perhaps not permit the garage such a prominent sign board, which seems to echo the traders' hanging emblems of earlier days. Retailing motor fuel from the kerbside would also perhaps be less acceptable: however, at the time, both 'Shell' and 'No. 1' Petrol at 1s/2d (6p) a gallon were readily available in the High Street. Another feature of High Streets of the time was the provision for the cyclist, and Elliot and Wade, a boot and shoe shop at no. 28 High Street, had racks for their customers' use. On the left of the photograph can be seen a sign advertising 'The Hut' refreshment rooms run by the Misses Alice and Louise Crocker at no. 15.

The Post Office c.1914

A new main post office for Weybridge had been opened on 8th February, 1914, on the corner site previously occupied by Portmore Park Farm, known as Webb's, after its last occupier. This was demolished in September 1912, allowing this impressive building, with a frontage of 65 ft. to the High Street and 88 ft. to Elm Grove Road, to be built. Also taken down at this time were some of the avenue of elm trees which once lined the main streets, although these were replaced with the three saplings in the picture. Provision was also made for a sorting office, telegraph room and telephone exchange. These new facilities superseded the existing post office in Heath Road. This post office in turn closed in October 1993 and was replaced by a franchise in Queen's Parade, Church Street.

Telephone Exchange c.1929

Before the later Post Office monopoly of inland telecommunications, Weybridge also had the facility of a telephone exchange provided by the National Telephone Company and housed at Avenue Villas, nearly opposite the G.P.O. equipment housed in the new post office. This telephone exchange, opened in March 1915, had a manual switchboard, possibly of Post Office type CBI, although Britain's first automatic exchange had opened at Epsom in 1912. Photographed c.1929 in the first floor room, telephonists under the guidance of their Supervisor, dealt with the area's calls. On the wall above her head can be seen the local police number, used for emergency calls before the introduction of the 999 system. A gradual increase in subscribers led to pressure on the facilities here and, in 1952, plans were published to build a new automatic exchange to increase Weybridge's capacity of 2,500 lines. This was duly built in Heath Road and opened in 1954.

High Street c.1914

This impressive panorama of the north side of the High Street was photographed from an upstairs window of Avenue Villa. Troops of artillerymen such as this one were a familiar sight in many parts of the country at this time, when millions of men serving the British war effort were on the move. This area was particularly used to troop movements: St. James' School in Baker Street was used as a billet for forces marching to Pirbright and Aldershot in the first months of the conflict. Perhaps the man leaning on a shovel was waiting to harvest the highway after the column's departure! Prominently situated on the corner of Elm Grove Road and boldly proclaiming the superiority of his wares was the shop of Walter Levermore, who had moved to his newly-built premises here in 1904. Originally a blacksmith in Queens Road, John Levermore established 'Holstein Cycle Works' in 1884 and moved to Weybridge High Street. Following the sale of the business in 1928, the site on the corner, no. 1 Holstein Parade, was used by radio and cycle dealers E. W. Farrow.

High Street c.1953

The growth of private motoring in the post-war era is well illustrated in this view of the High Street from the pedestrian crossing, marked by Belisha beacons. Weybridge's first sight of the new safety measure occurred during December 1938 when the distinctive orange globes were erected here. Named after the Minister of Transport, Leslie Hore-Belisha (1893-1957), the beacons were an immediate success in the effort to reduce the appalling number of road casualties then occurring. The distinctive facade of the Holstein Hall was to remain until 1963, while a new feature of the High Street was the erection of the four storey block "New Parade" in 1939. These 13 new shops replaced premises previously occupied by Edward Cocks' printing works and the group of private houses known as Avenue Villas.

38 High Street c.1905

H. Gatland's was a relatively short-lived occupation of the premises originally opened in 1897. His shop, operating from c.1902 to 1908, seems to be typical of the small grocers of the time, carrying a limited range of everyday foods and dealing mainly with the weekly wage-earners of the area. The 'Choice Tea' on offer would have cost the equivalent of just over 8p per pound.

52 High Street c.1908

In 1897 the Tappin brothers took over the lease of this shop, occupied from 1876 as a sub-branch of the London & County Bank and open for business from 10.00 a.m. to 3.00 p.m. two days a week, and ran their fruiterers' and greengrocers' business from here. The adjacent premises, no. 54, were also run by them from c.1902 as a restaurant until c.1913. Their delivery vehicles, a cart and a van, were included in the lease of the premises to the Lock family.

52 High Street c.1916

Alfred Lock took over the lease at 52 High Street in 1909 on behalf of his eldest son Edwin. The family had a market garden at Ash Farm, Shepperton, and had been established growers in the district since the late 18th century. Mr. Lock senior, wearing a moustache and trilby, can be seen by the pony's head, and his son Edwin, wearing a cloth cap, at their delivery cart's tail. The event photographed occurred in the middle of the first World War, when many basic foodstuffs began to be rationed. Weybridge people were actually queuing to obtain supplies of seed potatoes, the first planting traditionally taking place on Good Friday. As in the Second World War, the potato was to play a vital part in the diet of the nation, and a report in the local press in April 1917 records a woman fainting in the crowd outside a greengrocer's shop.

56 High Street c.1928

Ernest Rodgers had been in charge of Levermore's workshops, making 'the second to none' bike from steel tubing. By 1914 he had started his own business in Elmgrove Road and, following wartime work at Vickers, opened his new shop at 56 High Street in June 1924. An initial application to erect a petrol pump opposite the premises in the same year does not seem to have been successful, although in June 1928 the local authority agreed to allow the swing-arm fuel pump, seen in the photograph filling an assortment of containers. In December 1925 a new showroom for motorcycles was opened, the old shopfront of the previous occupiers, oil and colour merchants Brown & Son, being removed in one day. Ernest Rodgers' two sons Norman and Edward were also involved in the business. Norman was a pioneer in the new technology of radio and television and Edward became involved with model aircraft, having been a regular visitor to the aviation activity at Brooklands before the first World War. Norman Rodgers joined the business full time at the age of 15 in 1923, having been involved with radios since 1919. Wireless receivers were made on the premises, the setting up of the B.B.C. at this time creating a tremendous demand for the new sets, even though the larger versions could cost up to £60-70. The firm were also local pioneers of television, demonstrating a set using the Baird system in 1926 which gave an image 3 ins. square. Increasing business in telecommunications led to the family's opening a new showroom and workshop in the next-door premises at no. 58 during October 1930.

58 High St 1950

The summer of 1933 saw further demonstrations of the new medium when late night transmissions attracted large crowds. Further expansion in 1935 led to the acquisition of the adjacent premises at 60 High Street. The opening of regular B.B.C. transmissions on 2nd November, 1936 gave a further impetus to television's development. In the same year, the Rogers erected their landmark reception mast and continued to offer a comprehensive repair and retailing service. Post-war development of the business continued, and 1950 saw the opening of the fondly remembered model showroom. In the same year this crowd of Weybridge youth gathered to view transmissions from the annual trade show "Radiolympia".

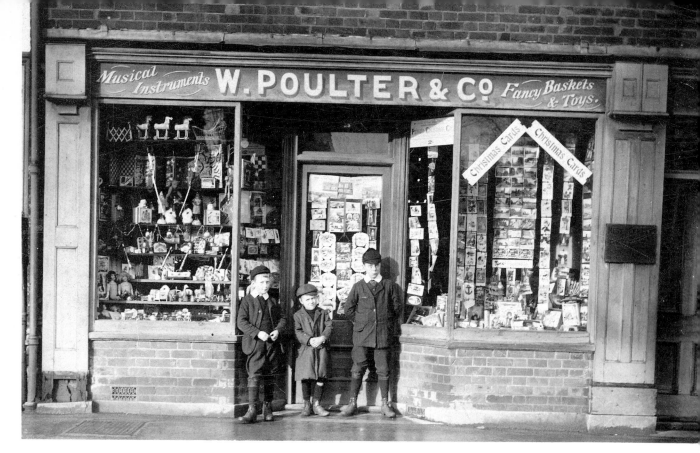

58 High Street c. 1910

This shop at 58 High Street had previously been run by Arthur Cooke, a basket maker. In 1901 William Poulter, originally a coachman to Judge Currey of Weybridge Heath, opened for business here retailing toys, musical instruments and postcards, etc., as well as the previous speciality. Mr. Poulter had a fine bass voice and was associated with local groups and the choir of St. Michael's, as were his sons, seen here. In 1912 he gave up the shop but continued as a teacher of music at Gascoigne Villas, Monument Green.

High Street 1900

Prior to the development of the Quadrant and other new parades of shops in Church Street, many of Weybridge's old-established traders were grouped near the Ship Inn. The premises of J.W. Rambridge, owned by the Friary Brewery of Guildford, had a distinctive porch which survived until 1969. Decorating the front of their shop and others in the High Street are the national emblems displayed as part of the town's Patriotic Procession and Carnival of June 1900. The sign proclaiming a welcome to 'Buller and the Surreys' referred to General Sir Redvers Buller and the Surrey Regiment, then on active service in South Africa. In the foreground can be seen the local horse-drawn bus offering a service between the railway station and the river.

The Ship Inn c.1950

Apart from its many links with sporting activities in the area, the Ship Inn, facing Monument Green, also has numerous associations with many types of road transport. As one of the larger establishments of its type in the village, and one able to offer accommodation to travellers, it became a stopping-point for coaches travelling to and from London. In 1839, for example, the 'Sovereign' en route from Addlestone called here at 8.15 a.m. A return journey the same day could be made, arriving at 7.15 p.m., having taken 3¾ hours. As well as facilitating travel to the capital, The Ship was a boarding point for local buses, and a complaint of 1925 recalled that The Ship had been a recognised stopping place for 45 years. These services, regulated by the Local Authority, charged 2d from the railway station to Monument Green and 3d to the river. The photograph illustrates some of the street furniture associated with the later London Transport use of the Ship forecourt, including the time clock by The Ship's signboard, the tubular steel shelter and the octagonal timetable display. Also seen on the right is the oak shelter, one of over 100 given to the people of Surrey by Mr. C.D. Strologo of Shamley Green in commemoration of the Silver Jubilee of King George V in 1935. Mr. Strologo, a native of Italy and ardent anglophile, wanted to provide protection for his fellow citizens from the cold and wet.

Monument Green c.1869

Weybridge's Monument Green area has been photographed on many occasions over the years, but this view appears to be the earliest thus recorded so far. The photograph was probably taken by the Richmond-on-Thames-based firm of A. & E. Seeley during a visit in the summer of 1869, when other parts of the village were also recorded. The village pump beside the Monument was at this time surmounted by a handsome lantern, possibly oil-lit, although a gas supply had arrived in the village in 1869, the same year in which a piped water supply, courtesy of the West Surrey Company, was laid to the area. Another pump on the same site was still working c.1910. The boys posing for the camera seem to be wearing typical school clothing of the period: perhaps they were pupils of Dr. Spyers' private school at Holstein House. On the left can be seen the shop and delivery cart of James Swayne, trading as a grocer and tea dealer at what was to become no. 1 Monument Hill.

Monument Hill c.1905

Large amounts of manpower were the order of the day for many of the infrastructure projects of the time. This group of labourers posed for the photographer during the laying of electric cable from the Thames Street generating station. Monument Hill itself was the first local road to be made up with the new technique of stone chippings bonded with the asphalt 'tarmacadaming'. Behind the men can be seen Smith's Monument Stores, the rebuilt successor to the original shop of James Swayne.

No. 7 Monument Hill c. 1910

William Reed had originally been employed as a stone dresser at Coxe's Lock Mill, Addlestone. This highly-skilled occupation became obsolete when the site converted to a roller mill c. 1900. However, Mrs. Reed was building up the business at Monument Hill which her husband's obituary of 1918 suggests had been started in 1885. Described as having 'an energetic existence', he had a family of nine children who also helped in the business by delivering newspapers. William Reed was a founder member of the Weybridge Urban District Council, where he was highly regarded for his independent views and as a champion of the working class. One of his daughters recalled the shop stocking claim forms for the Weybridge Charity and her father filling them up for potential claimants who would not apply for themselves. However, he would tear up any for those he felt were not really in need.

Monument Hill c.1950

Further evidence of the value of the photograph in recording the ever-changing face of our towns and villages is seen in this view of the foot of Monument Hill. The range of building styles, with their pegged, pantiled and slated roofline, well illustrates the greater wealth of period domestic architecture to be seen in the area until comparatively recently. Hill Foot Cottage, the posters in the windows of which marked it as unfit for habitation under the then current housing act, was demolished in 1956.

Monument Hill c. 1905

One of a series of photos taken by Herbert Philip Bassett for the Weybridge Urban District Council in support of its dispute with solicitor Oswald Milne. Some trees on his property, Old Orchard, were overhanging the highway and affecting the free passage of traffic. A scale on the left marked in feet illustrates the problem. The horse-drawn vehicles posed at the site represent two diverse local services, now wholly mechanised. Private horse-drawn omnibus companies were well established in many urban areas by the end of the 19th century, their use and fare structure regulated by the local authority. Weybridge's bus at this time, with a route from the Thames to the station via the Monument and Church, was owned between 1902 and 1906 by Arthur Winmill of Myrtle Cottage, Thames Street, and had been licensed to carry 26 passengers. Another important local service was carried out by the one horse-power 'tumbler' cart on the right. This was used to carry away the contents of those cesspits in use before the introduction of main drainage.

Royal Masonic Junior School c.1930

The original Masonic School for Girls was founded in London in 1789 at Somers Place East with the following objects: 'To receive under protection, for the purposes of Education, and during such period to maintain and clothe, the Daughters of and female children legally adopted by Freemasons of every religious denomination under the English Constitution who from circumstances arising from the death, illness or misfortune of either or both parents are reduced to a position requiring the benefits of the institution.' The junior school moved to Baker Street, Weybridge in 1918 with 45 girls under Headmistress Miss Harrop. Girls aged 7-11 were educated here until they moved to the other Masonic Girls' School at Rickmansworth Park, Hertfordshire. The pupils were evacuated from 1940 to 1946, the building being occupied by Unilever during their absence. After closure in 1974, the site was sold and developed as a housing estate.

St. James' School, Baker Street c.1912

Education for the majority of children meant attending one of the schools associated with either the Established, Roman Catholic or Non-Conformist Churches. Weybridge's St. James', on the site of the original Charity School, remained the largest of these. Under the watchful eye of their Master, possibly Basil Vokes, boys attend a 'manual training' class in woodwork. The log-book maintained by the Headmaster recorded in September 1906 that St. James' walls 'had been distempered a pale green, a great improvement on the bare bricks.' Although the facilities and conditions appear somewhat basic to those accustomed to carpeted and centrally-heated classrooms, the boys were given a good grounding in the use of hand tools and an understanding of the principles of craftsmanship. Additional tuition in woodworking skills was also available to the boys of St. James' and Oatlands Village Schools at the newly-opened Technical Institute in Churchfield Road.

CARSTAIRS

Weybridge Bowling Club c.1923

Weybridge is home to two centrally-located bowls clubs. That in Springfield Road is the oldest, having been founded in 1903 at 'The Ship'. A small group of keen bowlers started in the gardens at the rear of the hotel, where three rinks were laid out and a subscription of 5/- was agreed. The present headquarters was opened in 1922, when a new Cumberland Green of 42 yards square was laid mainly by the members. The club's pavilion, seen in the photograph, was opened the following year, but was destroyed by fire in 1967.

Baker Street c.1908

Looking east along Baker Street, we can witness the horse-drawn cart of a local tradesman being literally overtaken by 'progress' in the shape of one of the still-rare motor cars. Nevertheless the message on the back of the postcard reads: 'This is a view of the principal street in Weybridge. I do not like being here much after Woking – there is nothing to see!!' In the right foreground, in premises which still survive relatively unchanged, are the businesses of W.H. Cocks, picture framer and R. Cocks, stationer. Between them is the archway leading to no. 19, and beyond in no. 25 is the antiques and second-hand furniture shop run between 1906 and 1912 by A. Christy.

7 Baker Street c. 1880

The site of no. 7 Baker Street has been associated with local estate agents and auctioneers for the past 90 years, starting with John Bower Binns in 1903. Previously, William Howard's fishmonger's shop had been established here by c.1870 and members of the family had premises in Church Street and Oatlands Drive. Standing in the doorway to the right is Harry Howard, wearing the typical protective clothing of the period. The style of retailing from what appears to be a 17th century building is in strong contrast to that established in another Baker Street fishmonger's a quarter of a century later.

Tickner's fish Shop c.1905

These premises at 16 Baker Street, formerly occupied by Arthur R.H. Weston, draper, were taken by Arthur Albert Tickner in 1900-1901. He was issued with a game licence in August 1901 and the photograph suggests that this side of his business was as flourishing as the fishmongery. As was normal in the days before electrically chilled displays, the fish are arranged on a marble slab inside the shop to keep them as cool as possible. Many fishmongers took a great pride in the artistic arrangement of their wares. By this time, modern shops such as this one were also equipped with canvas blinds which could be lowered to protect the stock from sun and rain. The business was bought by John Lascelles c.1913, but reverted to its previous use when Baldwin's drapers shop at no. 14 expanded in 1915.

Baker Street c.1900

Street decorations commemorating royal events were a more regular feature of national life than in recent times. Weybridge and district was no exception to this trend, the massive efforts connected with the marriage of the Duke and Duchess of Albany being well recorded by the camera. It is thought that this view of the south side of Baker Street was taken when the whole area celebrated jointly the anniversary of Queen Victoria's accession to the throne and the occupation of Pretoria during the Boer War. Even the gas lamp posts were festooned for the occasion, this being the work of Mrs. Gammon and Mrs. Crawshaw. The photograph is also of great interest in showing the elevation of the old Weybridge Theatre, the second building from the left. This venture seems to have existed as early as 1751, and probably ceased theatrical activity c.1800. Subsequently used by a succession of bakers, and demolished c.1901, its site adjacent to the present Parkside Court is occupied by nos. 43-45 Baker Street.

Weybridge Welcomes Alcock and Brown, 18th June 1919

Heroes of the first successful transatlantic flight, Capt. Alcock and Lt. Brown were welcomed back to the town at a hurriedly-arranged reception at the Council Offices, which were housed in Aberdeen House. Following a visit to the Vickers Factory at Brooklands, which had built the converted Vimy bomber used in the crossing, a procession made its way to hear speeches from local dignitaries and Council officials. The assembled crowds were reminded that not only was the aeroplane built locally, but that it used propellers made in Addlestone, castings from Chertsey and was designed by the son of Chertsey's former Vicar. John Alcock was also a local boy, having lived in Weybridge before the War. Apart from the local pride in the achievement, the workers at Vickers were granted a day's paid holiday. Later, Alcock and Brown, knighted as national heroes, also presented £2,000 of their £10,000 prize money to those men at Vickers who had worked on their machine.

The Zenith 1913

Almost certainly photographed somewhere in the Weybridge area is this magnificent motorcycle, a product of the Zenith works, then established in the town. The company came to Weybridge from Finsbury, London at the beginning of 1909 and initially occupied premises at 1 Church Street. They were famous for the "Gradua" Gear System, which varied the diameter of the engine pulley and simultaneously corrected the belt length by sliding the rear wheel to or fro in the rear fork slots. The Weybridge-built machine illustrated was a 5-6 H.P. "V" twin with the newly adopted silencer. Highly successful at the time, the Zenith company also occupied premises at nos. 12 and 19 Baker Street, where bikes were produced until 1914, when the company moved to a larger factory in East Molesey, Surrey. Reportedly every locally-produced bike was road tested on the Brooklands track, its proximity being one reason for the arrival of the firm in Weybridge.

Sainsbury's, Church Street, 1922

J. Sainsbury's original shop, a dairy in London's Drury Lane, was opened in 1869 by John James and Mary Ann Sainsbury. Strict adherence to the principle of high quality and low price led to a gradual expansion outside London and the appearance of the familiar house style incorporating green and cream ceramic tiles and mahogany office screens in many provincial towns. The Weybridge branch opened in October 1920 in the premises previously occupied by grocers W. Coatman & Sons. This building was designed in 1891 by local architect J. Lindus Forge to replace the single storey shop of Edward Taylor Madeley which had burnt down. Madeley had a small chain of grocery shops in N.W. Surrey: that at Weybridge also included an off-licence. This was transferred to Coatman and gave Sainsbury's the facility to sell a range of wines and spirits, and for 40 years it was their only branch to sell alcohol. Sainsbury introduced grocery departments in their stores in 1920 and as well as familiar lines illustrated here offered a wide selection of 'own brand' groceries in addition to their usual range of dairy and meat products on which their reputation was built. The Weybridge branch closed in May 1973.

Technical Institute and Recreation Ground c.1914

This proud line-up of local horse power was possibly photographed on May Day. The Council's stables were then located behind its offices in Aberdeen House and it is thought that this string of draught horses had been prepared for the short-lived custom of decorating them for the May Day celebrations. In the background stands the new Technical Institute, opened on 7th November, 1912. Weybridge had an earlier Technical Institute situated in Elm Grove Road which had been opened in 1903. By 1910, however, the District and County Councils agreed jointly to fund the erection of a new building on land owned by the local authority. Constructed by the firm of S.J. Love of Sunningdale, the handsome building eventually cost £4,840. Its accommodation allowed for the manual training of children from local elementary schools, including woodwork for the boys and cooking and laundry work for the girls. Evening classes were also held in a wider range of subjects. The magnificent wrought iron gates which still adorn the nearby Churchfields entrance to the recreation ground were the gift of the park's donor Mr. John Lyle of sugar-refining fame, who lived at Finnart House. They had originally been one of two pairs set up at Bushy House, Hampton. When the park was first opened in 1908, they had been erected about 30 feet in front of their present position, to which they were moved c.1949.

Vigo House c.1925

For long one of the principal residences of the village, by the start of the 20th century Vigo House was home to Charles Augustus Lang and his son Dashwood, the pioneer propeller manufacturer. However, at the start of the first World War the building was the headquarters for a club for tradesmen and professionals. Following the end of the War, the pressure on the facilities offered at the Cottage Hospital led to discussion of the desirability of extending it or building on a new site. Initially, funds were provided by the Red Cross and local donations for rebuilding on the old site in Balfour Road to provide additional beds, a children's ward and X-ray department. However, lack of space made it impossible to proceed with the original plans. The Building Committee decided in February 1923 to recommend the construction of a new hospital on a new site, and collections began in order to provide the £14,000 estimated cost of the project. It was proposed to raise some £2,000 of this by selling the old cottage hospital site, but in the same month Hugh Locke King presented the hospital Management Committee with the Vigo House site. The house was demolished in March 1928 and the old hospital retained and renamed the Locke King Orthopaedic Clinic.

Opening the New Hospital 1928

By December 1924 tenders for the construction of the planned new hospital had been received from nine contractors, with that of £20,235 from Weybridge builder G. Jarvis being accepted. Local fund-raising continued, with donations both large and small coming from residents and organisations in Weybridge and the surrounding areas. A shilling brick fund, egg collections and the profits from local carnivals and fetes helped to raise much of the money required. Gifts in kind helped to equip the building, which received its first patients on 18th January, 1928, when the old hospital was vacated and immediately became the Locke King Clinic. The new hospital's official opening took place on 27th June, when H.R.H. Princess Beatrice performed the ceremony. Watched by a large number of the community, she received purses containing further gifts from some 50 local children.

Men's Ward 1929

Soon after the opening of the new hospital, it became clear that the intended Children's Ward included in the original plans had become an urgent necessity. The new hospital had treated 682 in-patients in its first year, of whom 259 were children. These were mainly tonsil and adenoid cases, but were treated in the adult wards. It was felt that the rise in the local population, coupled with a decrease in the fear of hospitals, could only increase the pressure on the local facilities. An Appeal Committee was set up to raise sufficient funds to build and equip the new ward. This was duly achieved and the ward opened on 31st October, 1930. Built at a cost of £6,300 and equipped for £700, it had five cots, five beds and a single-bed operation ward decorated in cream with panels depicting fairy tales.

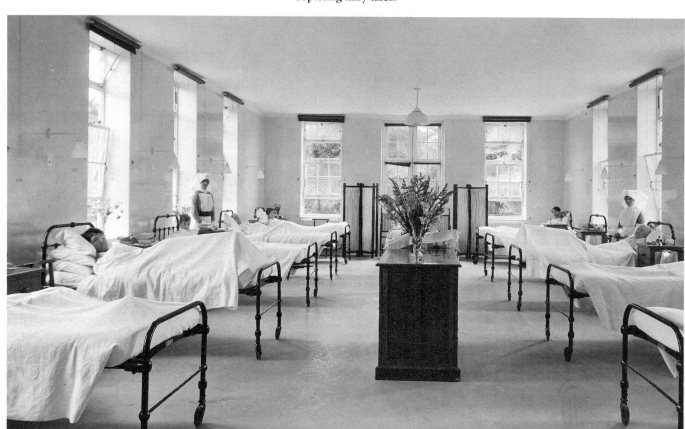

Queens Parade 1929

Originally built by local developer E.H. Thompson in 1899, part of the parade of shops was the home of one of Weybridge's cinemas. In 1912 a cinema had been proposed for the empty property, originally a grocer's shop. Following wartime use by Gordon Watney's engineering company, however, the Weybridge Kinema Theatre opened on 24th June, 1920, under the management of John Wiltshire, builder of the Holstein Hall. Refitted by Tarrant's in 1927 to provide seating for 520, it was acquired the following year by County Cinemas Ltd. and renamed King George's Cinema. In 1929, following the successful development of synchronised sound systems in Hollywood, the cinema introduced 'talkies' to the area when it showed 'The Singing Fool' for six days from 23rd September.

42 Church Street c.1908

Gems antique shop had opened in 1886 in the premises previously run as a grocers by Thomas Cooper. Cooper's daughters also ran a straw hat- and bonnet-making business from a side room which doubled as the family parlour. Harry Gems had originally been in the antiques business in Wigmore Street, London, and is remembered as being unable to read or write very well. However, the antique and curio trade carried on at the 'Old Curiosity Shop' was supplemented by a range of related repair and restoration services, such as rivetting china and glass at 2d per rivet, and the sale and hire of bicycles, accessories and Bath chairs. Other contemporary stock included cannon, ploughs, statues and a man-trap. Not visible in this photograph but a particular feature of the facade is the window made from a large recycled picture frame. The building itself is listed by the Surrey County Council as being of architectural interest and is thought to be of 16th or 17th century date with alterations. The contemporary photograph of the back parlour illustrates well the antiquity of the building, with the low ceiling accentuated by what are almost certainly re-used timbers. A memoir of the late 19th century recalls four or five stone steps down to the back parlour which was so dark as to have paraffin lamps permanently lit. Electricity had by this time been installed to illuminate what was perhaps a slightly atypical interior, probably furnished with a variety of shop stock.

Weybridge Parish Church 1869

Weybridge's original medieval church, which stood slightly to the south of the present building, was demolished in 1849. Replacing the two-aisled structure with wooden belfry, the present church was built to the design of the architect J.L. Pearson the previous year. It was originally designed for a congregation of 608, but the area's growing population necessitated enlargement in 1864, and again in 1889 to provide seating for 900. The pointed Gothic-style building included a spire 150 ft. high, which became the dominant feature on the local skyline and was illuminated for the first time on 8th May, 1945. The church's ancient graveyard, already virtually full by the time the photograph was taken, contains a wide range of tombstones and memorials. Reflecting the wide spectrum of parishioners from nobility to local traders who found a common resting-place, the inscriptions in the church and churchyard have been transcribed and published by the Walton and Weybridge Local History Society.

St. James' Church 1875

The parish church received a new peal of eight bells in 1875. These were the gift of Mrs. Anna Farr Roberts and her children, Miriam and Chevalier, in memory of her husband Henry of The Limes, Church Street. The largest bell, the tenor in the centre of the photograph, was suitably inscribed by the makers of the peal, Taylors of Loughborough. This peal superseded the previous ring of three bells, and the general practice of recycling the old metal consigned bells of 1597, 1614 and 1798 to the melting pot. Following concern first expressed in 1968, a new steel supporting frame was made by the Whitechapel Foundry to replace the original wooden one and the bells were re-dedicated on St. James' Day 1989.

Weybridge & Oatlands
This map is reproduced from the 6 in. Ordnance Survey map as revised in 1894-95 and published in 1897.

Weybridge Cottage Hospital c.1912

Now refurbished and named Locke King House, Weybridge's original hospital opened its doors to patients in July 1889. Following a public meeting the preceding year at which it was decided to combine a cottage hospital and parish room, a building fund and committee of management were established. The site for the building in Balfour Road had been acquired from Hugh Locke King; the building and its furnishing cost around £1,600. Although designed for nine beds, its initial accommodation was limited to four regular beds and another for emergencies. Later building work increased its capacity to 14 by converting the original parish room in the building to form a women's ward. Initially, only medical cases were admitted, emergency operations being carried out in the wards. Local residents requiring such treatment at the time would be operated on in their own home, the doctor's house, or sent to London or Guildford. The photograph also shows the hospital's notice-board, giving details of visiting hours (between 2 and 4 p.m.), the 10 m.p.h. speed limit sign and the front of the yard of builder George Jarvis, established here in 1879.

Weybridge c.1925

Croydon Airport-based Surrey flying Services produced a range of aerial views of many parts of the county in the years following the first World War. The techniques perfected for military purposes were utilised to provide views for general sale. This summertime shot neatly illustrates the wealth of historical detail to be gleaned from such photographs. At top left, the line of the 1865 Wey Bridge clearly demonstrates the problems which the refusal of Peter Locke King to sell part of his land caused with the alignment of the new bridge. The ancient settlement grouped around the parish church and new shopping facilities contrasts with the more recent development of the Portmore Park Estate, seen top right, with its large detached houses and extensive tree cover.

A Wey Bridge Bus Crash 1929

A spectacular accident completely stopped road traffic over the Wey Bridge for two hours on the afternoon of Sunday 5th May, 1929. The bus, a London General Omnibus Company vehicle on route 162 from Slough to Leatherhead, had skidded on the wet road. After spinning round and catching Augustino Petrucci's Ford ice cream van, it came to rest as illustrated. Although the back of the bus was practically ripped off, only five passengers sustained minor injuries.

Wey Meadows c.1890

Mowing a fine crop of meadow hay with scythes, the two agricultural labourers are actually working on the Addlestone bank of the Wey. Although machinery was in common use for many agricultural purposes by the mid-19th century the use of manpower was still particularly suited to marginal and awkward areas of land. Both men appear to be wearing typical working clothing of the period: hats of all types seem to have been universally worn, while the trousers were tied below the knee as a precaution against both dust and rodents disturbed during harvesting.

The Quadrant 1900

Weybridge took the opportunity of both celebrating Queen Victoria's Coronation Day of 28th June and fund-raising for the widows and orphans of local men killed in the Boer War. The occasion was marked with a huge procession of decorated floats and wagons accompanied by brass bands and six local fire brigades. No fewer than 111 entries took part in the parade round Weybridge and Oatlands, collecting contributions on the way. Many fine photographs were taken on the day. This particular one shows 'H.M.S. Powerful', a battleship, crewed by local tradesmen and their children under 'Admiral' H. Bennett. Mr. Bennett traded from 9 The Quadrant as the 'Empire' confectioners. At no. 1 The Quadrant, Thomas Dix's butcher's shop – newly built in 1897 – was to remain until 1915.

Autotrix Works c. 1912

In 1911 a three-wheeled light car was being produced in Weybridge. This enterprise was set up as a result of a partnership between George Wadden, who ran a ladies' hairdressers at 13 Church Street, and S. Edmunds, who had been Manager of the Limes Parade branch of Walter Levermore, cycle dealers. Its workshops and staff of ten were located in five stables in Quadrant Yard. By April 1911, examples of their work were being raced at Brooklands under the brand name Autotrix. Two models were available, one powered by a 3½ h.p. single-cylinder JAP engine with belt drive, or an 8 h.p. twin-cylinder version with gearbox and chain drive. The chassis as seen here could then be fitted with a variety of types of bodywork, including wickerwork, allowing for one- or two-seater versions. Up to 30 of these three-wheelers were built at Weybridge until the partnership ended when Edmunds left for Sydney, Australia, and the company's stock and machinery were sold in July 1913. George Wadden, however, persisted with the cycle-car concept and moved to Cobham in 1914 in partnership with Mr. West to build the four-wheeled Simplic model. After the first World War, Wadden returned to Weybridge and had works in Jessamy Road until c. 1923.

Church Street c.1939

The basic townscape of this part of Church Street is little changed today and all the properties visible are included in the present conservation area. At no. 3 The Quadrant, Lush and Cook, Cleaners & Dyers, previously trading from Heath Road, had been in occupation since 1916. Saddler and sports goods dealer James Barrenger operated next door in premises originally run as a dairy. His neighbour at no. 1 The Quadrant, Savory's clothiers, had erected the impressive square-faced clock in November 1932. The illuminated electric clock was also originally used to mark the stopping place for buses.

Weybridge Literary Institute 1873

A photograph taken at the opening of the building. The gift of Peter Locke King to the Weybridge Mutual Improvement Society and Literary Institute, it was opened on 1st February 1873. A contemporary report of the event describes how the walls were covered with very large pictures presented by Mr. Benjamin Scott of Heath House, and that it was capable of holding 500. The opening ceremony enabled one Hodgson Pratt to tell the assembled company that the building and associated activities 'allowed the working class to extricate themselves from the demoralisation of public houses (cheers)'. Also used by the Weybridge Fire Brigade from its foundation in 1874 until the building of the Fire Station in Balfour Road in 1881; since 1900 the hall has been home to the Constitutional Club and now the Conservative Club.

The Quadrant c.1912 and c.1953

In the intervening 40-odd years between these photographs being taken, a variety of changes had occurred in the area of Quadrant Green. A seat had been provided by the local authority in 1928, although most of the elm and lime trees had been cut down. The provision of a public telephone call box near to the existing post box recalls the position of a sub-post office at no. 39 Church Street until c.1929. The original posts and chains around the Green had been erected in 1910. Further evidence of the changes in the transport scene are also evident. The Douglas motorcycle, just visible outside Luxford's contrasts with the 500cc B.S.A. Twin parked outside the premises of the major motorbike dealers Lewis and Sons. Mr. W.L. Lewis was the son-in-law of Walter Levermore, whose family traded from Limes Parade between 1910 and 1987. This was a branch of Walter Levermore's existing shop in the High Street, shown on page 14.

Church Street c.1912

This view looking north from outside Stainton's premises was taken on the same day as the photograph at the top of page 38. The large canopy beyond belongs to Thomas Dix's butcher's shop, the proprietor of which lived on the premises and, from 1897, also ran the pork butcher's opposite. The latter shop was sold to the Addlestone Co-Op in 1919. At one time Mr. Dix was the only butcher in Weybridge, and Mr. Charles Day, who worked as a roundsman for him for nearly 40 years before retiring in January 1931, would visit 50 or 60 houses a day, memorising up to 40 orders at a time! Beyond Dix's on the left is the ironmonger's shop run by Harold Stanley Marsh from 1908, which sports a distinctive Yale key sign advertising the locks on sale within, and an impressive array of garden tools outside.

Quadrant Green c. 1925

In the more leisurely days of the 1920s, the lorries and car shown here were restricted to 10 m.p.h. by the red speed limit sign seen as a dark band round the lamp-post. The posts and chain edging the Green had been erected in November 1910. In the same year Limes Parade, behind, had been built on the site of the timbered house, The Limes, demolished in 1909. Three of the original occupants can be seen here still in business. Ainslie Bros., butchers, in no.3 Limes Parade, had closed during the first World War, but re-opened in September 1919 under the management of Mr. W. Stephens. In no. 2 is Tom Thomas, tobacconist and confectioner, while no. 1 is occupied by Frederick Briggs, hairdresser and Post Office. The Union Cartage Company van was no doubt calling at the furniture depository built in 1908 for John Stainton of Oatlands. The business was taken over in the mid-1920s by H.F. Luxford, previously a fruiterer at no. 82, opposite, but he retained the name Stainton's for some years.

Curzon Road c.1905

Another of the Weybridge Urban District Council's services to its ratepayers is seen in action. The occasion for the photograph, taken outside the recently-built houses in Curzon Road, was probably the local custom of dressing working horses for May Day which died out during the first World War. For the purpose of rubbish removal, Weybridge and district had originally come under the Chertsey Rural Sanitary Authority, which had used private contractors to collect household refuse and the contents of cesspits. At the time this picture was taken, the Council Rubbish Depot was located in Walton Lane and the horses stabled in Elm Grove Road. A memory of c.1910 also refers to seeing two cart horses at Oatlands Farm resting after pulling the dustcarts. The nature of household rubbish at the time would have varied greatly from today's. Most houses burnt coal, which formed clinker and ash, many bottles were returnable and there was far less packaging of goods. This method of collection also allowed for the easier retrieval and recycling of useful items. Local collection does not seem to have been mechanised until 1938, although Moore's of Baker Street had asked to demonstrate a Fordson tractor and trailer to the Council in 1927.

Rose Cottages c.1910

These four cottages on the Heath were originally erected in 1785 for use as Weybridge's Poorhouse until 1835, when the inmates were transferred to the new building at Ottershaw, itself now converted to private housing. The local parishes grouped together to form 'unions' for the purpose of administering the Poor Laws. Weybridge with others formed the Chertsey Union, whose Board of Guardians sold the now surplus premises to Peter Locke King in 1839. One of the inhabitants at the time the photograph was taken recalled that the Heath in front of the cottages was used to market geese at Christmas time. The birds would be driven up from Sussex and sold to the local poulterers. Mr. Lovelock also recalled seeing bullocks sold on this area, having arrived by train at Weybridge Station.

The Cemetery Chapels and Lodge, Brooklands Lane, 1876

A gradual rise in the population of the Parish of Weybridge led to pressure on the ancient graveyard around St. James'. On April 24th, 1875, the Burial Board agreed to accept the tender of local builder and undertaker Samuel Woods to erect chapels and a lodge for the sum of £1,560. The picture by local architectural photographer George Ward shows the completed buildings in 1876. Its original area of three acres was extended by a further four purchased from Hugh Locke King at £500 an acre in 1920. The new facility was overseen by Henry Tilly and his wife as Lodge Keepers, who were paid £20 a year to maintain the ground and chapels and keep the gate. For digging a common grave and sounding the bell, the parish sexton was paid 4s. under the scale of charges agreed in 1873.

The Mitre c.1910

Thought to have been built c.1860, the Mitre was described in a rating valuation of 1910 as an Inn, House and Stables occupied by William Roberts. In the 1892 Return of Licensed Premises, The Mitre's patrons are recorded as being gardeners, presumably from the many large private estates then existing in the area. Kingston-on-Thames brewers Hodgson held the lease from the owner, Mrs. Eliza Lord, but in July 1912 they purchased the freehold for £3,900 from her executors at auction. During the construction of the Brooklands Racetrack, The Mitre is reported as having supplied gin and whisky to some of the labourers via a nine-year-old errand boy.

Catholic Church c.1910

Weybridge's Roman Catholic congregation seems to owe its origin to the establishment of a prominent Roman Catholic, Philip Southcote, at Woburn Farm in the adjacent parish of Chertsey. Southcote's widow endowed a chaplaincy on the Woburn estate. Bridget Southcote died in 1783 and the local community was served by a succession of local priests. In 1815, however, when the estate was bought by the non-Catholic Admiral Sterling, the Rev. Peter Potier moved to Weybridge, where he continued to serve the local Catholic congregation in his own house until 1834. The church in Heath Road owes its existence to James Taylor, a rich property-owner of Islington, London, who retired to Weybridge and built the original chapel in the grounds of his house. This was dedicated on 4th November, 1835, and became the sacristy of the later church, built in 1881. Dedicated to St. Charles Borromeo, the building became famous as the resting-place of several members of the French Royal Family in exile in Britain, the original vault built for members of the Taylor family being used for King Louis Phillippe and Queen Marie Amélie, who had come to live at Claremont in Esher, and worshipped here.

Post Office Staff 1905

The entire staff of the Weybridge Post Office posed for a group photograph in the grounds of the old Post House situated on the corner of Heath Road and Elgin Road. Seated at the front are the telegraph boys who could have started work at age 13, the lady telephonists, office staff and postmen. As well as the distinctive uniform, a number of them can be seen wearing stripes on their chests, each band representing ten years' service to the Post Office. The man in the centre is thought to be the local Postmaster of the time, Mr. Charles Woodley.

Weybridge Sorting Office c.1910

A sorting office was also housed on these premises, and many of the cards used in this compilation would have been handled here. At the time the photograph was taken, the main Weybridge office not only delivered the post four times a day but also cleared its box no fewer than 17 times between 2.30 a.m. and 9.00 p.m. This level of service enabled a ½d stamped postcard to become the universally popular medium for sending messages before the first World War. The Heath Road premises became a branch office when the new Post Office in Weybridge High Street opened in 1914.

Brooklands House c.1930

Built for Peter Locke King, the house was occupied by members of his family between 1862 and 1936, when Dame Ethel, the widow of Peter's son, Hugh, sold the property. During the First World War the house was made over for use as a hospital, which operated between October 1915 and October 1919. As a result of her tireless efforts for the Red Cross, she was made a Dame of the British Empire. The aerial view usefully illustrates the house and part of the grounds, including the extensive and comprehensive greenhouse and kitchen garden area. Typically of gentlemen's estates of the time, the household could thus be almost self-sufficient in a wide range of general and more exotic foodstuffs. During Hugh Locke King's time, the estate had its own brickyard, and even the iron gates were made on site. After the Second World War the house became the campus for Weybridge Technical College (now Brooklands College), which opened in 1948 with 12 staff and 118 part-time students. These were mainly apprentices on day-release courses from Vickers and other local firms, thus continuing the connection between the track and later aeronautical manufacturers and the rest of the estate.

1st Weybridge Girl Guides 1910

Weybridge was home to one of the very first Boy Scout troops in the country, formed as the 1st Weybridge (Brooklands Own) in 1908. Hugh Locke King gave the group permission to use the woods on his Brooklands estate for their tracking and camping activities. Following lobbying of Lord Baden Powell by girls who attended a Scout rally at the Crystal Palace in 1909, a youth movement for girls, the Girl Guides, was formed. This group also used the woods at Brooklands and posed wearing their green tunic uniform and straw hats.

Back row left to right: D. Caulder, D. Bullen, Miss Janes (Capt.), H. Crapp, C. Tilley, A. Scragg, E. Robertson. Second row: A. Puttock, D. Hewer, M. Greenfield, A. Levermore, B. Tickner, N. Steadman. Front row: W. Clark, C. Preece.

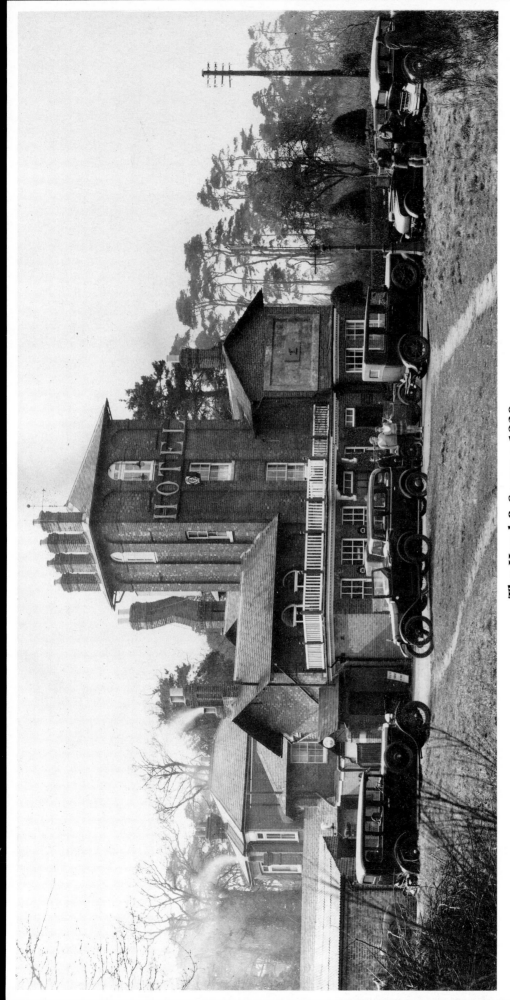

The Hand & Spear c.1930

Weybridge's distinctive Hand & Spear Hotel may have grown out of private building, possibly a summer house or shooting box erected for the new owner of the Brooklands estate. The purchaser, Lord King, Baron of Ockham, took possession of his lands in 1830 but died in 1833. Prominently featured in the large panel on the right of the building is the King family crest, from which the hotel took its name. The arrival of the railway and station in 1838 seems to mark the change of use and the building rapidly became one of the principal hotels in the area with extensive facilities for patrons and their horses. A later venture of the Locke King family, the opening of the Brooklands track south of the railway, brought increased business. In July of 1907, it was reported that over 100 cars were placed on the Heath in the vicinity of the station while their passengers and chauffeurs went to the races nearby. The track's continued popularity between the two World Wars made the Hand & Spear a favourite meeting place for both drivers and spectators.

Weybridge Station c.1912

First opened in 1838 to serve the new London to Southampton Railway, Weybridge Station has seen many changes to its layout and amenities. Rebuilt as early as 1857, the structure seen here reflects the major alterations carried out at the beginning of the 20th century. As part of the extensive work involved in adding a fourth track to the line from Waterloo, a platform which stood in the present space between the up and down lines was removed. As well as work on the track, a new booking hall and offices were built. Also built between 1902 and 1905 was the present pedestrian overbridge and the long slope to the downside platform. This replaced a flight of 60 steps which had long been a source of complaint by Weybridge commuters. Also replaced were the goods lifts, originally hydraulically operated. The handsome new booking hall in the photograph was extensively renovated in 1985 in a refurbishment of the whole station costing c.£250,000. However, as a result of an arson attack on 5th January, 1987, it was badly damaged and subsequently demolished and rebuilt.

Weybridge Station c.1930.

The station was also a popular venue from which to observe a wide range of local and main line services. Here a Maunsell U 1 Mogul class unit steams past the goods shed demolished in 1966. The Southern Railway line to Portsmouth was electrified in 1936, and the main line platforms 2 and 3 were extended in 1966 to accommodate 12 car multiple-unit trains.

Station Road c.1920

The route laid out across Weybridge Common at the time of the local enclosure c.1804 was designated a through road and made 40 ft. wide. Its original name of Hanger Hill, from the Old Anglo-Saxon place name meaning 'a wooded slope', was no doubt changed soon after the arrival of the railway in 1838. However, after local lobbying the name officially reverted to its original form by 1933 when, following the formation of the new Walton & Weybridge U.D.C., it was altered to avoid confusion with the Walton street name. The photograph by Chertsey photographer Thomas Gadd is one of a series of local views taken during the summer of 1920. The cottages in the foreground have since been demolished, making way for Pyrcroft Lane.

Hanger Hill c.1935

Halted on the freshly-gritted road outside no. 34 is William Sharp's delivery van. Sharp, a baker, was based at 45 Queens Road for 40 years between 1899 and 1939. Pupils of the Hall School in Prince's Road recorded details of local tradesmen's horses in 1934. Sharp's cart was reported as being pulled by Tommy, a red roan and very good-tempered! In the right foreground is the corner of Pine Grove. No. 32, in the left foreground, was once the lodge of Charles Churchill's mansion, Weybridge Park, and later the sanatorium of Weybridge Park College.

Churchfields Avenue c.1930

Facing west along Churchfields Avenue in 1930, St. James' Church could be clearly seen across the recreation ground. The houses on the right, with no. 10 at the edge of the picture, are largely unchanged, although in the intervening 60 years the saplings in their front gardens have grown into mature trees. Behind the palings on the left are the playing fields of Wallop School, then under the management of Mr. Allen G. Roper. The south-eastern part of the Avenue, between here and the school, was developed as part of the Weybridge Park estate.

St. Michael's Church, Prince's Road c.1910

Erected as a chapel of ease to the Parish Church in Church Street, the church of St. Michael and All Angels was built in 1874 to the design of architect William Butterfield. Its site in Princes Road was reputedly on that of a gravel pit. The area's growing population at this time necessitated its construction, but falling congregations led to its becoming redundant and it was demolished early in 1973. Its interior as shown on the contemporary postcard was described by Philip Palmer, the ecclesiastical tourist from Guildford, in 1910. Lit by electricity, its pews of stained pine could accommodate 550. He also noted the choir of 14 boys and six men (who sat on oak pews), and the central east window depicting the Nativity. Other stained glass executed by Nathaniel H.J. Westlake was saved at the time of demolition and is preserved in Elmbridge Museum.

Wiltshire's Machine Bakery c.1890

John Wiltshire's bakery business had opened on Hanger Hill about 1881 in premises originally built for one Augustus Thesiger. By 1887 Wiltshire was advertising himself as 'Confectioner, Cricket Common and Monument Green'. In 1903, however, the bread making business was disposed of and he concentrated on the work of catering, cooking and confectionery. His function catering seems to have led him into owning and managing public halls and cinemas in Weybridge with varying degrees of success. The Hanger Hill premises, having been converted into showrooms, were sold in 1919 and again in 1927, by which time the building had been renamed York House. Mr. Wiltshire, seen here wearing a boater, died at the age of 78 at his Portmore Park home in 1935. Apart from the delivery vehicles, the photo is of interest in showing on the right one of Weybridge's first electric street lights, which had been installed by March 1890 attached to a series of poles around the area and were supplied with alternating current from a generating station in Church Walk.

Recruiting Rally 1915

In an effort to swell the ranks of His Majesty's Forces, Weybridge hosted the local section of the Great Recruiting Rally on 2nd October, 1915. Large crowds gathered to watch the parade, which started from Weybridge Station, headed by the Surrey Guides in their smart green tunics under the leadership of Commander Pager R.N. Members of various military and civilian organisations followed. Members of the Volunteer Training Corps of Chertsey, Addlestone and Weybridge were photographed parading on the Cricket Common. Afterwards the procession marched to Old Palace Gardens to take part in military sports, while the Holstein Hall was crowded that evening when a programme of war films was shown. The outcome of this splendid effort was one new recruit from Weybridge!

Temple Market c.1930

As well as developing the Weybridge Park and High Pine estates, Edward Thompson was also responsible for Weybridge's distinctive Temple Market shopping complex. Originally opened as a single storey lock-up retail outlet for his Walton Park Nurseries, the open area in front displayed flowers and garden accessories. The name is thought to derive from an enquiry as to whether the whitewashed building with green glazed tile roof was a temple or a market. Mr. Thompson then decided to call the premises Temple Market. Under this name he further developed the site and in 1932 gave details of a major rebuilding to provide ten shops and residential accommodation. Widely advertised in the local press of the time, many features of the complex were publicised, including free parking for 60 cars and the promise that 'only first-class traders are being accepted'.

Oatlands Drive c.1905

Further work to link Walton-on-Thames with an electricity supply generated at Weybridge power station was carried out in 1905. This gang were laying ceramic conduits to house the 2,500-volt cable supplied by the Callender Company. The firm, founded in 1882, developed the familiar insulated cable from their original manufacture of road surfacing material made of bitumen from Trinidad. Further early cabling work along Oatlands Drive occurred in August 1912, when permission was granted to lay a telephone line from Chertsey to Walton, also via Weybridge High Street and Monument Hill.

New Zealand Auxiliary Hospital, Oatlands Park, c.1918

Thought to have been built by the 7th Earl of Lincoln, and later the country home of the Duke and Duchess of York, Oatlands House passed into the hands of the South Western Hotel Company, while most of the Park was sold off for the development of Oatlands Village, begun in the early 1850s. In 1915 the premises were taken over for use as the no. 2 New Zealand Auxiliary Hospital A. The maximum capacity of the hospital was 800, in addition to the 1,200 who could be accommodated in the Second New Zealand General Hospital at Mount Felix, Walton. The whitened stones edging the drive, typical of army camps, are here varied by the addition of five forcing pots for rhubarb or sea-kale. The camp effects were auctioned in October 1919, and the hotel finally reverted to the ownership of the Oatlands Park Hotel Co. Ltd. in December, but damage to the premises was found to be extensive. Liquidators were appointed, and £10,500 was received from the War Office in compensation, but £20,000 was spent on redecoration and refitting before the Hotel re-opened on 30th July, 1920.

The Broadwater c.1906

Oatlands' Broadwater lake had long served as a place of recreation in both summer and winter conditions. The body of water, nearly a mile long, seems to have served in the 19th century as a repository for Weybridge town's sewage. In 1875, however, the Inspector of Nuisances was able to report that the offending pipe had been cut off. By the turn of the century, one neighbouring property had a boat house on its bank and a petrol motor boat to cut the weeds on the lake. It was also reportedly used by swans for breeding, and it teemed with moorhens and other aquatic species. The cleaner waters also provided excellent pike fishing. When frozen, the lake became a popular venue for ice skating, with local boys earning money for supplying chairs and assistance with putting on skates.

Oatlands Farm c.1936

Dairy farmer Thomas Higgs operated from Oatlands, Greenlands and Broadwater Farms, Grotto Road in the 1930s until he was bought out by Job's Dairy in 1939. Both horse-drawn and hand carts were used. Mr. Kilminster, seen here, delivered milk twice daily on a round covering the whole of Queens Road. The handsome new handcart is loaded with crates of the relatively newly-introduced re-usable glass milk bottles – a great advance in hygiene over the old practice of dispensing milk from the churn into the customers' own jugs. Patrons of at least one local dairy had had new-style delivery for some time. In April 1925, Weybridge Creameries had advertised their milk at 5d a quart, delivered twice daily after 6.00 a.m. in sealed glass bottles.

Oatlands Drive c.1909

Henry Shaw's drapers and boot dealers business had premises on both sides of Oatlands Drive when this photograph, looking north-east towards Walton, was taken by the Teddington firm of Young & Co. On the right, the prominent gas lanterns over the windows of what is now (1993) Sunflower Reprographics illustrate not only the sparse street lighting of the time but the necessity of illuminating shops when late night shopping was the accepted norm. Long working hours for the majority kept shops open until 8.00 or 9.00 at night. Window shopping could at least take place on Sundays or the local early closing day of Thursday, which changed to 1.00 p.m. instead of 2.00 in 1906. These premises were taken over c.1929 by Nellie & Edith Osborn who traded as ladies' outfitters. Shaw's other shop, on the left, is now occupied by Pollington's Newsagents.

Oatlands School, 1924

William Swallow, the highly-regarded Headmaster of Oatlands School from 1921 to 1938, is seated in the centre of this group, with the Mistress, Miss E. Shaw, on his right and the Infants' Mistress, Miss Whitburn, on his left. This building, erected in 1882 to accommodate 130 pupils, had housed the boys from 1883, while the girls and infants had continued to be taught in the original school of 1850, now St. Mary's Village Hall. In 1922, however, the later building had been altered and the girls and infants moved here, creating a mixed school with infants' department.

Unusually for an official school group, the children have been photographed in the road – an arrangement perhaps impossible in today's traffic conditions. On the left of the picture is the Headmaster's house, where Mr. Swallow lived with his family.

Anderson Road 1911

The coronation of George V on 22nd June, 1911, was the occasion for patriotic displays like this one in streets throughout the country. Some of the local children have posed for the photographer in front of the flags and bunting in Anderson Road, which is thought to have been named after its builder. The houses shown here were built between 1846 and 1859. Beyond, on the right, is The Prince of Wales public house, opened in the 1860s and, at this time, run by Frank Gibbins. Outside stands a horse-drawn delivery cart from the Windsor brewers, Neville Reid & Co.

Oatlands Drive c.1915

Looking south-west towards the Flint Gate public house, one sees Henry Ward's shop in the right foreground. Formerly a gas engineer in the 1880s, then a blacksmith and farrier, Ward had by this time turned his hand to plumbing. Another tradesman who later seized an opportunity to diversify was Herbert Frederick Luxford, whose shop appears here on the left. Having operated for some years as a greengrocer at Oatlands and The Quadrant, in the mid-1920s he bought Stainton's upholstery and furniture removal business, which had premises conveniently situated close to both of his own shops.

High View, Oatlands Drive c.1910

The home of Ernest Hill and his family was captured in these photographs of the rear of the house and its superb morning room. Its formal flower beds and manicured lawns, so typical of plantings of the period, were the product of full-time gardening staff without the benefit of powered machinery.

From the elaborate gas-lit pendant light fitting to the draped fireplace, the camera also provides an invaluable record of the style and furnishing of a wealthy local house of the period. The Hill family were reputedly the first in the area to buy a Rolls Royce car. To enable him to drive and maintain it, they sent their coachman on a course and kept him on as a chauffeur.

Oatlands Chase c.1912

Developed as a high-class residential street in the late 19th century, by 1912 Oatlands Chase boasted about 24 villas such as those in the photograph. One, 'Penn', had a brief claim to fame when in 1898 the owner, Edward Jeffery Venables, rented it to the novelist Emile Zola for five guineas a week. Zola, having fled from France, had been staying at the Oatlands Park Hotel under the name of M. Pascal, but called himself Jacques Beauchamp when he moved into 'Penn' on 1st August, 1898. His stay lasted less than four weeks, as he so disliked Mr. Venables' taste in furniture that he moved to 'Summerfields' in Spinney Hill, Addlestone on 27th August. By 1912, 'Penn' was in the hands of Walter Henry Morseby. The house still survives on the south of the road as no. 24.

Castle Road c.1930

As seen from Oatlands Chase, Castle Road has changed little since this view was taken, and remains a quiet residential side street. Castle Green and Charlton Kings, however, had yet to be developed. The distinctive turreted roof of Rockgarth (at this time known as Haddon), on the corner of the road, can be seen on the right beyond the now-vanished sewage ventilation pipe.

Oatlands Avenue c.1910

This view shows the quiet, tree-lined Avenue known in the 19th century as 'America', on account of its fancied resemblance to the forest scenery of that continent. It was a popular walk with local people, but by 1910 many of the trees and rhododendrons had been sacrificed in the building of houses such as those on the left in the photograph above, near the corner of St. Mary's Road. This road had been known as Balls Road until 1882. On the near side of the Avenue, a sewage ventilation pipe (which still survives in 1993) is also serving as a lamp-post and a convenient resting-place for a bicycle. Further off is a delivery cart belonging to Arthur Edwards, a Queens Road butcher.

Oatlands Close c.1930

Edward Thompson's building of the Close, part of the High Pine estate, had begun in 1924, and when he had taken up residence at 'Westernhay' he advised prospective purchasers that he was architect, builder and surveyor of the development. It was built as a private street, and Mr. Thompson advertised that the necessary road materials could be excavated on the spot – an important consideration before the surface was tarmacadamed. No two houses in the Close were to be exactly alike, and none were to cost less than £700.

Weybridge 1928

Another high-level aerial view of the area, this time one of a series taken by the Aerofilm company during October 1928. As well as demonstrating the impressive railway cutting required to accommodate the London and Southampton Railway's route to the south coast, many other features of interest can be seen. The Queens Road area of Weybridge was well established as a shopping centre and was still dominated by the 90-ft.-high spire of the Congregational Church, built in 1865. Also well developed by this time was the High Pine Close estate and its associated roads, formerly the estate of Mr. G. Ferguson and called The Hollies. Although it was never built, the year following the taking of this photograph saw a petition to the Southern Railway for a new station near to Haines Bridge. In the lower right-hand corner can be seen the house and grounds of the property named Swiss Cottage, later developed as Woodland Way.

Queens Road 1944

Members of the 3rd Surrey (Weybridge) Battalion of the Home Guard pause for refreshment during their efforts to clear up bomb damage at "Netherby", Queens Rd. The house and grounds had been taken over at the beginning of the Second World War in 1939 by the Electric Furnace Company of London, the house being owned by the firm's chairman. In 1944 a German Flying Bomb, the V.1., landed on the stable block shortly after the staff had left. The company remained here until 1956 when it moved to Sheerwater. Subsequently demolished, the site was developed as Netherby Place.

Queens Road c.1910

This through route had at last, in the stretch maintained by the Weybridge Urban District Council, been made up by this time. In May 1905 it was decided to dress the road surface with boiling tar and limestone. The pavement seems to have been made up in 1909, when both Queens Road and York Road were laid with an artificial stone. Both types of local bicycle delivery noted on pages 10 and 41 are represented here: the telegraph boy on the left certainly seems to have been at the lower age limit for full-time work, and only just of a size to ride his non-geared Post Office-issue bike.

Queens Road c.1925

Alfred Bannister had set up in business as a draper at 40 Baker Street in 1902, and in February 1912 opened his second shop at 105 Queens Road which, according to the 'Surrey Herald', 'bids fair to become the finest shopping part of the locality in view of the impending development of St. George's Hill'. The new premises built by W.A. Annett of Walton had a granite facing and a main shopping area of 85 ft. x 40 ft., with mahogany shop fittings and polished oak floor. It was equipped with a private telephone service to the Baker Street store. In February 1929 the business was re-organised, gowns, coats and millinery being sold exclusively at the Queens Road premises; while 40-42 Baker Street became 'The Silk Shop', also selling soft furnishings. In September 1939, Bannister decided to close the Baker Street outlet and transfer its stock to Queens Road. At no. 103, on the corner of South Road, R.A. Burningham had opened a grocer's shop in December 1910. The grocery trade is still carried on here by Cullen's.

The Duke of York c.1910

Posed for the Elmgrove Road photographer Berriman Bolton are the family of licensee Ernest Nye. Designated as a beerhouse with an area of 25 perches in the contemporary rating valuation, the house was named after a previous owner of the land which once formed part of the Oatlands Park estate. The Duke of York seems to have been opened in the 1860s, and replaced with the present building in the 1920s.

Queens Road c.1950

Looking north along Queens Road, the busy retailing character of this part of the street can be clearly seen, with a typically wide variety of shops. Next to E.M. Waldie's corsetry and underwear shop are Barwicks, tobacconists and stationers. This family had been in business in the area for a long time, Samuel Barwick having had a grocer's shop at 12 York Road by 1874, which had become a newsagent's and post office by 1911. In 1928, George and Kate Barwick established a second shop here at 59 Queens Road. The Westminster Bank had opened their Queens Road branch in 1923, while Dale's Garage had been catering for the rising numbers of motorists since the early 1930s. In the distance on the right can be seen the Odeon, built in the distinctive style of the 1930s at a cost of £14,300, to seat 912 people. It opened on 9th April 1934, and enjoyed an enviable reputation for comfort. After the Odeon chain took over the County Cinema in 1939, the two venues shared a newsreel, which necessitated regular rapid cycle rides by the projectionist from Church Street to Queens Road, often arriving just in time! After closing on New Year's Eve 1960, the Odeon was converted, becoming St. Martin's Roman Catholic Church, now demolished.

Triumphal Arch, Queens Road 1882

Standing between the Post Office on the left and the Congregational Church on the right, this was one of three triumphal arches erected in Weybridge to celebrate the wedding of the Duke and Duchess of Albany. Prince Leopold, youngest son of Queen Victoria, married Princess Helen of Waldeck at St. George's Chapel, Windsor, on 27th April, 1882: triumphal arches were erected at intervals along their route from Windsor through Old Windsor, Chertsey and Weybridge to Claremont in Esher, where their honeymoon was to commence. Mr. and Mrs. Webb, who ran the Post Office, organised a fund for the erection of the arch outside their premises and were able to present all the children of the village with a bun and an orange out of the proceeds. The arch was built by Mr. Smith and decorated with flowers, evergreens and flags by Mr. Povey, gardener to Mr. Gillespie of Elgin Lodge, and Mr. Chapman of Oatlands Park Nursery. The small fir trees beside the road were provided by Admiral Egerton of St. George's Hill. On the far side was the inscription: 'Long Life and Happiness'. Sadly Prince Leopold, a haemophiliac, died in 1884.

Field Place Estate c.1932

The site of the Field Place estate of the Yool family is now occupied by Northfield Place, Kingswood Close, Southfield Place and Crossfield Place. On the death of Mrs. Yool, widow of prominent Weybridge resident and local benefactor Henry Yool, Col. G.A. Yool sold the grounds for development. The new estate, built by the Addlestone builders E. Clarke & Sons, was started in mid-1932, with detached houses on offer from £1,495 to £2,100. The builders also advised prospective purchasers that 'the estate is completely protected against encroachment or inferior development'.

St. George's Hill c.1905

Many residents of Weybridge and the nearby areas of Addlestone, Cobham and Byfleet became familiar with the delights of walking along the wooded paths of the Egerton family estate before its development. Although there were frequent complaints about visitors straying on to private walks and preserves and leaving litter, the majority of tourists to the hill were well behaved and had much to enjoy. As well as the birch and bracken depicted in the photograph, the wide range of flora and wildlife to be seen is recorded: one memoir recalls snowdrops, primroses, bluebells and even two or three bee orchids. Also to be seen were wild deer, hunted on occasion by Mr. Hutchinson Driver from Horsell.

St. George's Hill, Brooklands Road Entrance c.1930

The house on the left of the photograph, now called 'Long Barn', was built by Tarrant as an entrance lodge and later extended. It was designed by the noted architect Blair Imrie, who was also co-winner of a competition for the Royal Horticultural Society building at Wisley in 1909. The house was one of the first erected on the new estate and was built soon after approval by the local authority on 3rd June 1912. Framed by the neo-Tudor brick arch, perhaps inspired by the original local example remaining from Oatlands Palace, is the notice reminding visitors that St. George's Hill was a private estate.

Tarrant's Plumbers 1912

Some of the large work-force used for the construction of the new residences on the Hill posed for the photographer. This group of tradesmen and apprentices were plumbers or gas-fitters. As is typical of group photographs of the period, the men pose with the tools of their trade and wearing their working clothes of bib-and-brace overalls and, in most cases, a flat cap. The gentleman in the centre is almost certainly their foreman, wearing his bowler hat. Tarrant's men on the development worked a ten-hour day from 6.00 a.m. to 5.30 p.m., with meal breaks Monday to Friday, and from 6.00 a.m. to 1.00 p.m. on Saturday. Labourers at 6d (2½p) per hour through to thatchers at 1s. (5p) per hour worked to a system, building three houses at a time with a gang of about a hundred under a foreman.

St. George's Military Hospital c.1916

Originally opened on 2nd October, 1913, as the clubhouse for the new golf course, by October 1914 this had been converted into a 60-bed hospital for the growing number of War casualties. Members of the club had subscribed over £1,500 to convert and equip the building for the purpose, and between 1914 and 10th March, 1919, the hospital treated some 3,000 wounded soldiers. Disaster struck the Tarrant-built clubhouse on 18th March, 1920, when a fire broke out in the thatched roof. Despite the efforts of local fire brigades, the conflagration rapidly took hold and the building burnt down to the walls. It was subsequently rebuilt with a flat roof and one storey fewer.

St. George's Hill Lawn Tennis Club c.1930

Tarrant's original plan for the development of the estate did not include a tennis club. The area subsequently used was to be built on as an 'Old English Village' to house the gardeners and chauffeurs necessary to maintain the lifestyle of the estate's new inhabitants. This was not proceeded with and on 7th June, 1913, the St. George's Hill Lawn Tennis and Croquet Club was opened by Prince Alexander of Teck. Originally laid out with eight grass and two hard courts, the Club also provided two croquet lawns and a bowling green. Warren Pond was stocked with rainbow trout and could be used for boating and bathing. Although originally planned to be built in 'log cabin style with reed thatched roof to harmonise with the surroundings', the clubhouse was actually constructed in brick, while the thatched roof proved short-lived and was burnt out after a fire in March 1918. Reconstructed with a tile roof, the new clubhouse re-opened on 25th July, 1921.